DATE DUE

APR 0 5 2019			

Everything
You Need to
Know About

Crohn's
Disease
and
Ulcerative
Colitis

Diseases of the digestive tract like Crohn's disease or colitis are sometimes crippling, but staying positive and informed can help immensely.

Everything You Need to Know About

Crohn's Disease and Ulcerative Colitis

Sandra Giddens and Owen Giddens

The Rosen Publishing Group, Inc.
New York

Published in 2004 by The Rosen Publishing Group, Inc.
29 East 21st Street, New York, NY 10010

First Edition

Library of Congress Cataloging-in-Publication Data

Giddens, Sandra
Everything you need to know about Crohn's disease and ulcerative colitis / Sandra Giddens and Owen Giddens.
p. cm. — (The need to know library)
Includes bibliographical references and index.
Summary: This book describes Crohn's disease and ulcerative colitis, explaining the theories on the causes of inflammatory bowel diseases as well as the symptoms and treatments for these various diseases.
ISBN 0-8239-3996-0
1. Inflammatory bowel diseases—Juvenile literature.
[1. Inflammatory bowel diseases. 2. Crohn's disease. 3. Diseases]
I. Giddens, Owen. II. Title. III. Series.
616.3'44—dc

Manufactured in the United States of America

Contents

Chapter *1*   What Is IBD?   6
Chapter *2*   Treatment   27
Chapter *3*   Coping with the Stress   42

Glossary   54
For More Information   57
For Further Reading   59
Bibliography   60
Index   61

Chapter 1

What Is IBD?

It's awfully embarrassing to talk about. I mean I am a teenager and I want to live a normal life and do what all the other kids are doing. I don't want to tell everyone the life history of my bowel problems! It is so hard to discuss diseases like ulcerative colitis and Crohn's disease, which cause inflammation in your digestive system. Some of the symptoms are very embarrassing to talk about—not dinner table conversation! Most of the time I can carry on in my life just like everyone else, but there are times when I am in so much pain that I have to remain at home, close to a toilet. Sometimes I have to be hospitalized. Medications help me most of the time. I know that Crohn's disease and ulcerative colitis are common and affect one hundred thousand Canadian men, women, teens, and children and an estimated one million people in the United States. I also know that anyone, regardless of age, gender, or race, can get inflammatory bowel disease. Unfortunately, I am the one who has been affected by the disease. The medical profession still does not know the causes of IBD, and they don't have a cure as yet. I can only be strong, manage my medications and symptoms, and maybe even help others understand what I am going through.

Crohn's disease and ulcerative colitis are two similar yet distinct conditions that are often referred to as inflammatory bowel disease (IBD). On meeting people with either Crohn's disease or ulcerative colitis, you could not detect that they have anything wrong with them. IBD does not manifest itself like measles with the well-known signs of rash and fever. On the outside everything looks normal. But it is inside the body—in the digestive system—that inflammations are festering and eruptions are occurring. These diseases can cause the intestines to become inflamed, form sores, bleed easily, and form scars on the normal smoothness of their inner lining. IBD is also known by other names, such as Crohn's colitis, ileitis, distal colitis, and pancolitis.

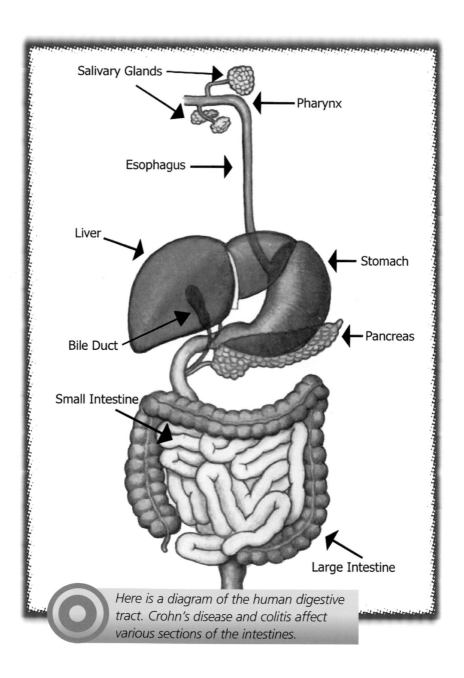

Here is a diagram of the human digestive tract. Crohn's disease and colitis affect various sections of the intestines.

IBD is found throughout the world, more extensively in North America and northern Europe. It also appears in the Middle East, central Europe, and Australia. The lowest frequency of reported cases has been in Asia and Africa. One might conclude that IBD appears to exist predominantly in temperate rather than tropical climates. IBD is more common in people with white skin and more prevalent in Jewish people.

The Digestive System

In order to understand IBD, it is a good idea to have a health lesson on the digestive system. The digestive system refers to all the organs involved with the digestion, absorption, and metabolism of nutrients. The purpose of the digestive system, also called the gastrointestinal (GI) tract, is to extract calories and nutrients from food and to absorb the protein, sugar, and fats into the body. This provides the body with the energy it needs to be active and grow. What is amazing about the human body is how complex each system is and how the systems coordinate so beautifully together, as if each part was a section in a symphony orchestra. Each body part has a function and plays a role in making beautiful music. When they work automatically without any problems, a symphony of nature emerges and it is miraculous. But when problems occur, the breakdown can affect the whole working order of the human body.

Imagine you are traveling through the digestive system. You would be in a continuous tube beginning from the mouth, through the esophagus, the stomach, the small bowel (small intestine), the large bowel (colon), the rectum, and ending through the anus. The mouth smashes and crunches up food, which makes it easier to swallow. The esophagus is a straight, hollow tube that carries food and fluids from the mouth to the stomach. The stomach is a large pouch that receives food from the esophagus, stores it, mixes it with digestive juices, dilutes it, and delivers it slowly to the small intestine. The small intestine, or small bowel, absorbs the nutrients. The small intestine of an adult is 18 feet (6 meters) long and about 1.2 inches (3 centimeters) in diameter. Can you believe that you have that much intestine inside you? It coils up like a snake to fit into the abdominal cavity. Terms used to describe the general segments of the small intestine are the duodenum (the upper 10 centimeters), the jejunum (the rest of the upper two-thirds), and the ileum (the lower one-third). Digestive juices from the liver and pancreas enter the duodenum and mix with food. As food passes through the jejunum and then the ileum, it is digested and absorbed, while the remaining undigested food, which is liquid, is passed along to the

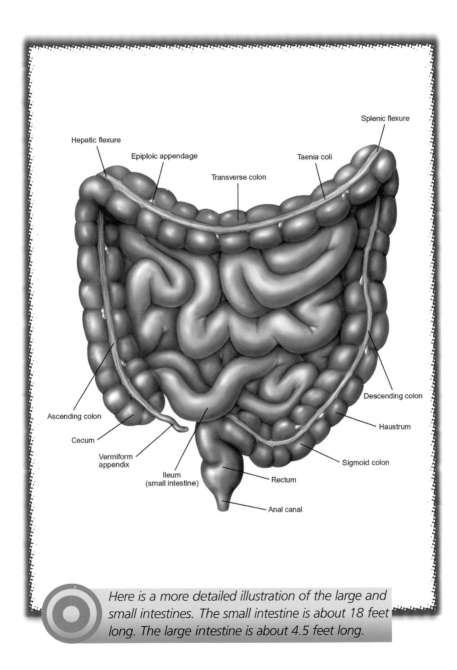

Hepatic flexure

Epiploic appendage

Transverse colon

Splenic flexure

Taenia coli

Ascending colon

Cecum

Vermiform appendix

Ileum (small intestine)

Rectum

Anal canal

Descending colon

Haustrum

Sigmoid colon

Here is a more detailed illustration of the large and small intestines. The small intestine is about 18 feet long. The large intestine is about 4.5 feet long.

large intestine. The large intestine (large bowel) is wider and much shorter than the small intestine. The main part of the large bowel is the colon and the lower end is the rectum. The colon is about 4.5 feet (1.5 meters) long and runs up the right side, across the abdomen, and down the left side. The major function of the colon is the absorption of further water and salt so that the remaining undigested food becomes solid. Once digestion and absorption have been completed in both the small and large intestines, solid waste (stool, or feces) remains, which is stored in the rectum and eliminated from the body through the anus (a bowel movement).

Why did you need to know all of that? The answer is that to really get into the gritty facts about IBD, you need to become acquainted with the digestive tract, especially the small and large intestines. You also need to know that when these digestive inflammations occur, you can be affected both physically and emotionally. IBD is particularly difficult for teens since it can affect a person's self-esteem, body image, and lifestyle at a time when "being like everyone else" is so important.

Crohn's Disease

If you look back on the history of Crohn's disease, there appears to be a number of recorded cases of people who

had the symptoms of the disease but were not diagnosed. In fact, the condition did not even have a name
until Dr. Burrill Crohn, a New York City doctor, began to
study it. It was 1930. He was a doctor at Mount Sinai
Hospital, and he was very concerned about his
seventeen-year-old patient. The young man's symptoms
were high temperature, abdominal pain, diarrhea, and a
lump in the appendix area of his body. The young man
was operated on, and it was discovered that the lump
was a hard mass of inflamed tissue at the lower end of
the small intestine, the ileum. In 1932, after more
research in this area, Dr. Crohn presented a medical
paper on this disease and subsequently Crohn's disease
was named after him.

Crohn's disease is particularly prevalent in North
America, western Europe, and Australia. Crohn's
disease has its peak onset in adolescence and early adult-
hood, between ten and forty years of age. It has only
been recently discovered that the onset of Crohn's disease can be in children under age ten and adults over age
sixty. Crohn's disease can affect any part of the gastrointestinal (GI) tract, from the mouth to the anus. It is a
disease in which the walls of the intestine become sore,
inflamed, and swollen. Patches of inflammation can
occur with healthy tissue between the diseased areas.
Crohn's disease can cause abdominal pain, diarrhea,

fever, and loss of weight. Some people even have pains in their knees, ankles, and other joints. Crohn's disease is called ileitis when it is in the ileum, Crohn's colitis when it is in the large intestine, and ileocolitis when both the small and large intestines are involved. Crohn's disease sometimes involves other parts of the digestive system, too, such as inflammation of the mouth, esophagus, stomach, duodenum, appendix, or anus. Crohn's disease is a chronic condition that may recur at various times over a lifetime. Some people have long periods of remission, sometimes for years, when they are free of symptoms. There is no way to predict when a remission can occur or when symptoms will return.

Ulcerative Colitis

Medical experts have found documented cases of ulcerative colitis as far back as 200 years ago. Unlike Crohn's disease, which can affect any part of the digestive system, ulcerative colitis affects only the large bowel (or colon) and only a single layer of bowel tissue. Ulcerative colitis causes ulceration and inflammation of the inner lining of the colon and rectum, while Crohn's disease is an inflammation that extends into the deeper layers of the intestinal wall. Ulcerative colitis almost always starts in the rectum and can extend as a continuous inflammation from there into the rest of the colon. When ulcerative colitis affects only the lowest part of the colon, the rectum, it is called ulcerative proctitus. If the disease affects only the left side of the colon, it is called limited or distal colitis, and if it affects the entire colon, it is called pancolitis. The inflammation makes the colon empty frequently, causing diarrhea. Some of the main symptoms are bloody diarrhea, abdominal pains, and occasionally pains in the joints. Studies show that as many as 20 percent of patients with ulcerative colitis have a close relative with either ulcerative colitis or Crohn's disease. Researchers continue to look for specific genes involved in the cause of both diseases, but at the present time no one can predict which, if any, family member will develop IBD.

What Are the Symptoms?

Here are some typical responses from young men and women who suffer from this type of disease:

I was having diarrhea, and many times I had an urgency to have a bowel movement, but nothing came out. I was always feeling bloated with a lot of gas. There was a lot of mucus in my stool.

It was grade six and I had already missed half the school year [from] being ill. I had terrible stomachaches, and I was continuously losing weight. I was very pale. At first my knee was really swollen, then my ankle. At times during the night, I could not physically get up to walk to the bathroom because my joints ached so much. I had bloody stools and diarrhea. I remember my dad buying a Coke and a bag of chips and I could not eat it.

People who have Crohn's disease can have many different symptoms depending on where the disease is acting up. Some of the most common symptoms are abdominal cramping, often in the lower right side, diarrhea, and weight loss. Other symptoms can include nausea, vomiting, bloating, and canker sores. Some people get a distinct swelling in the abdomen. There may also be rectal bleeding, sores around the anus, fever, swelling, or pain in the joints. Bleeding might be persistent, often leading to anemia (low red blood cell count). Children can suffer from delayed development and stunted growth.

People with ulcerative colitis usually have bloody diarrhea. The diarrhea may begin slowly or quite suddenly. There can also be abdominal pain and fever as well as skin lesions and pain in the joints. There are times when the rectum is inflamed and undergoes spasms. This may cause an overwhelming feeling of having to go to the toilet and eliminate the bowel, but although the urge is there, nothing happens. This is called "false urge." Weight loss and poor growth occur less often with ulcerative colitis than with Crohn's disease.

The following chart shows the similarities and differences between Crohn's disease and ulcerative colitis.

Crohn's Disease	Ulcerative Colitis
Any part of the gastrointestinal tract, from the mouth to the anus, can be affected.	All or part of the colon (large intestine) is involved.
Inflammation may be present in all layers of the bowel wall.	Inflammation is present in the inner lining only.
Inflammation is discontinuous through the digestive tract, with inflamed bowel separated by healthy segments.	Continuous inflammation occurs from rectum and up a distance.
Symptoms: diarrhea, abdominal pain, loss of blood, diminished appetite, weight loss, weakness, fatigue, nausea and vomiting, fever, and anemia.	Symptoms: severe and bloody diarrhea, abdominal pain, poor appetite, weight loss, nausea and vomiting, mild fever, anemia, and the loss of bodily fluids.
Surgery may be necessary and helpful, but is not a permanent cure.	Removal of the large bowel is generally the prescribed cure.

With IBD, you may have to go to the bathroom frequently. It is possible that you may go to the bathroom
dozens of times a day and throughout the night. The
anus can hurt from going repeatedly to the washroom as
well as constantly wiping yourself. There are many different degrees of IBD. Some people have mild cases, while
others have more severe cases. IBD can come and go quite
suddenly. Some people experience the symptoms only a
few times, while other people have many more episodes.

What Causes IBD?

At first, the medical community considered food allergies
or intestinal bacteria to be the causes of IBD. Some spec-
ulated that psychiatric disorders were linked to IBD. At
this point, however, no one is certain of the cause of IBD.
We do know that it is not contagious. It is not passed on
as a common cold can be. IBD is not caused by stress or
by food. In some instances, more than one member of the
family has IBD, but this is not always the case. Members
of the medical profession and scientists continue to
actively work to find both the cause and a cure.

IBD is a chronic disease, which means that people
have it all their lives. The symptoms and severity of
IBD vary considerably from person to person, but for
most individuals the condition follows a pattern of
causing only the occasional problem, then flaring up for

a while before subsiding again. People do not usually die from IBD. Most of the time sufferers lead normal lives doing the same things that other people do, like going to school, working, getting married, and having children. People with IBD try to lead a regular life, just like everyone else.

There are many theories as to what causes IBD. One theory is that the immune system, which normally protects you against disease, may be working too hard in the intestine. The immune cells in the intestine protect you from unhealthy bacteria. There are many chemicals in the body that signal the immune cells to increase or decrease inflammation. These chemicals usually provide a careful balance of protection. For some reason, this balance is lost in people who have IBD. In other words, the immune system becomes overactive in the intestine, resulting in inflammation.

There are also many theories about what causes Crohn's disease, but none has been proven. One theory is that some agent, perhaps a virus or bacterium, affects the body's immune system and causes it to trigger an inflammatory reaction in the intestinal wall. Although there is a lot of evidence that patients with this disease have abnormalities of the immune system, members of the medical profession do not know whether the immune problems are a cause or result of the disease. However, doctors believe that there is little proof that

Crohn's disease is caused by emotional distress or an unhappy childhood. Crohn's disease affects males and females equally and appears to run in some families. About 20 percent of people with Crohn's disease have a blood relative with some form of IBD, most often a sister or brother, and sometimes a parent or child.

> *My sister has colitis, and she ended up having surgery. The doctors always thought I had irritable bowel syndrome when I was in my teens. It wasn't until I was older that I was diagnosed with Crohn's disease.*

There is a tendency for children and other relatives of people with IBD to develop these conditions as well. This may be because there is a genetic predisposition. Women with Crohn's disease who are considering having children will be comforted to know that the vast majority of such pregnancies result in children without IBD. Research has shown that the course of pregnancy and delivery is usually not impaired in women with Crohn's disease. It is always a smart idea for a woman to discuss her concerns with her doctor before pregnancy, however.

There are many theories as to what causes ulcerative colitis as well. The most popular theory is that the body's immune system reacts to a virus or bacterium by causing ongoing inflammation in the wall of the intestine. People who have ulcerative colitis have abnormalities in their immune system, but again doctors do not know if this is a cause or result of the disease. Ulcerative colitis is not caused by emotional stress or sensitivity to certain foods, but these factors can trigger symptoms in some people.

Complications

Although no one wants to dwell on the complications of IBD, there are many conditions that can result from it and they need to be investigated thoroughly. Be aware of the complications but do not fear that any or all will necessarily happen to you.

Two complications of IBD are malnutrition and malabsorption. Malnutrition is when there are not enough nutrients in the body. Malabsorption is the inability of the body to absorb certain nutrients. Malabsorption can happen when nutrients are lost through bleeding and diarrhea. It can also occur when some medications taken for IBD interact adversely with nutrients, as well as when part of the intestine is surgically removed. There may be less absorptive tissue to process the nutrients in food.

Since people who suffer from IBD can experience severe pain, the result can be poor appetite. Sometimes people

IBD is a disease that is very difficult to talk about. Having an understanding friend can help.

with IBD simply do not feel like eating. When a person does not eat, it can lead to a feeling of exhaustion, extreme tiredness, and weight loss. It is essential that children and teens with IBD keep on eating so that they will keep on growing. One major concern for children with IBD is growth. If you became sick with IBD as a child, you might be shorter than others in your class. There is no true understanding of why this can occur, but it is possible that young people, especially those with Crohn's disease, might eat less food than their bodies need, either because they are not hungry or because eating causes the pain and diarrhea to get worse. When less food is eaten, the body is not provided with sufficient nutrition to promote growth. Therefore, it is important to eat enough calories for good growth. Children with Crohn's disease who have not been treated can have poor growth or might not enter puberty as early as their friends and classmates.

People with IBD often have hemorrhoids (swelling of the rectal or anal veins) and fissures (cracks in the skin in the anus). These can usually be treated with over-the-counter medications. There can also be a concern when breaks in the inner lining of the bowel deepen and develop into tracts, therefore resulting in abscesses (infected boils) and fistulas (abnormal openings between organs, or from an organ to the skin's surface). These problems can be treated with antibiotics and, if more serious, with surgery.

Another complication of IBD is when the lower intestine (ileum) becomes so scarred and narrow that food becomes blocked and can't pass through the intestine. This can be dangerous, and surgery may be needed to alleviate the problem.

The most dangerous complication in ulcerative colitis is toxic megacolon. This is caused when the colon swells up because of an accumulation of gases. If a perforation occurs in the bowel at the same time, the bowel's contents, which include bacteria, can get into the abdominal cavity. Toxic megacolon can be fatal unless corrected with surgery.

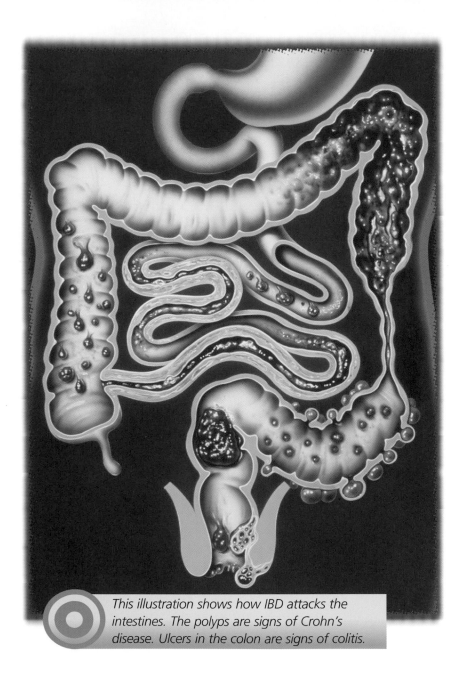

This illustration shows how IBD attacks the intestines. The polyps are signs of Crohn's disease. Ulcers in the colon are signs of colitis.

There is also an increased risk for people who have had ulcerative colitis for more than ten years of developing colon cancer. The risk continues to increase, so annual diagnostic tests are recommended.

Another area of concern for IBD patients is increased risk for osteoporosis (bone loss). Bone density scans may be recommended by your doctor. Inflammation of the joints and eye disease can be further complications from IBD. Arthritis and joint pain can affect up to 20 percent of people with IBD. Sometimes the joint pain is present only when the disease flares up, and sometimes the arthritis is independent of IBD. A doctor might prescribe arthritis medications. Patients with IBD are also at an increased risk for blood clots in the leg veins. This can be serious and needs to be investigated. Sometimes patients are put on blood thinner medications.

Lactose intolerance is more common in people who have Crohn's disease. Milk and milk products containing lactose can cause cramps and diarrhea. Sometimes, people supplement their diet with lactose-free products or take lactase enzyme tablets before eating milk products. Lactase enzyme tablets, which help people digest foods containing lactose, are available at the drugstore without a prescription.

It is worth repeating that all or even some of these complications do not necessarily happen to everyone with IBD. They might not happen to you, but any concerns should always be talked over with your doctor or medical specialist. There are more and more diagnostic measures being developed that are less invasive to the body. Medications have been known to ease and comfort people with IBD. You should not deny your symptoms, and you should not suffer needlessly. There is help, and you should actively seek it. The longer you wait, the greater the chance of further complications.

Chapter 2

Treatment

Even though doctors do not know what causes IBD, they can help people feel better by alleviating their symptoms. They can support the person suffering from IBD by giving advice on the day-to-day problems of living, like how to eat properly. They can prescribe medication and perhaps recommend an operation. A doctor who is an expert on IBD and other digestive system problems is called a gastroenterologist, although many family doctors also treat IBD. IBD can be managed through nutritional therapy, medications, surgery, or a combination of all these treatments.

Food

I have tried different diets. I have been on all liquids to flush my system out. I have been nose

fed. When I am having a severe case, even a piece of toast is hard to eat. I don't eat a lot of greasy food. My body, for some reason, cannot tolerate microwave popcorn.

There is no special diet for people with IBD. From time to time, certain diets, like low-fiber, high-fiber, low-sugar, and dairy-free, become the latest rage or trend, but not one has been proven to have real benefits. Sometimes, people with IBD find that certain foods can make them feel worse, and there are times when they do not want to eat anything at all. The food they manage to eat may not stay in their bodies long enough (due to frequent diarrhea) to give them the proper nutrition they require. Sometimes raw foods like salads can cause trouble if your intestine is narrow and inflamed or if you are experiencing diarrhea. If you are taking the medication prednisone, it would be beneficial to avoid salt, especially in junk foods. A doctor might recommend a dietician who can support you in eating properly. At times, supplementary nutrition may be recommended. This nutrition is in liquid form, so the bowels do not have to work extra hard to digest it, thereby giving the bowels time to rest. Some supplements are drunk like a milkshake (and can be vanilla or chocolate flavored), while in others, the liquid food is pumped through a tube directly into the stomach. The tube is inserted either through the nose or through a special hole that doctors have made in the stomach. These feedings are usually done while you are sleeping. They can be done in a hospital or at home.

> *I could not eat, so they started tube-feeding me. They put the tube into my nose and then food went right to my stomach. This gave my bowel a rest. Let's face it, I was in grade six and I was hooked up to this tube at night. It was real annoying, but truthfully, I did not mind it. I was being fed this way while I was sleeping. I even hooked up the nose tube myself. It was no big deal for me. I needed it!*

If you are experiencing severe gas, you should avoid the following foods:

Lima beans	Cauliflower	Brussels sprouts
Cabbage	Apples	Onions
Turnips	Cantaloupe	Soybeans
Cucumber	Navy beans	Watermelon
Honeydew	Corn	Green peppers
Kidney beans	Broccoli	Avocados
Dried fruits, like dried apricots or prunes		

If you are experiencing severe diarrhea, here is a list of actions you might take to improve how you feel:

◎ Avoid caffeine products like soda pop, tea, coffee, and chocolate.

◎ Reduce your intake of fiber (bran).

◎ Reduce the amount of lactose (milk products) you consume.

◎ Drink a lot of clear fluids (eight cups of water a day).

◎ Make sure you are getting enough potassium in your diet.

◎ Make sure you are getting enough sodium in your diet.

◎ Avoid fatty foods.

◎ Avoid spicy foods.

◎ Avoid eating too much sugar.

◎ Eat small meals, but eat them frequently.

◎ A good vitamin supplement would probably be recommended.

◎ If severe diarrhea continues, talk to your doctor about medications.

Medicines

I have taken an anti-inflammatory drug every day for the past seven or eight years. I never had to take cortisone. I have a mild case. If I don't take the anti-inflammatory drug, the diarrhea flares up again. The pills are very expensive! I always wonder about the long term and how the medication is affecting me, but I still take the drugs because the alternative is worse.

There are many medicines recommended for people with IBD. There is always the good and the bad when dealing with medications. The good is that they help to eliminate the symptoms that cause you severe discomfort, but the bad is that many of these medicines have side effects. People with IBD can take over-the-counter or prescribed medications to reduce inflammation in their digestive tracts, to reduce symptoms of cramping and diarrhea, and to treat any complications that may arise.

Here are some medications used to treat symptoms of IBD:

◎ **Sulfasalazine**

Used to treat mild to moderate attacks of IBD. It reduces inflammation and

diarrhea. It has been used for more than fifty years to treat IBD. It significantly reduces the chance of flare-ups. It can be prescribed indefinitely. Side effects can include nausea, reduced appetite, vomiting, stomachache, and skin rashes.

◉ 5-Aminosalicylate (5-ASA)

Used to treat mild to moderate attacks of IBD. It decreases inflammation, reduces diarrhea, and may also prevent flare-ups. Side effects are the same as for sulfasalazine but are less common.

◉ Glucocorticosteroids (Steroids)

Prednisone is prescribed frequently. Steroid medication is used to treat moderate and severe attacks of IBD. This medication reduces inflammation. There are a number of side effects, including increased appetite and subsequent weight gain, increased energy, less need for sleep, moodiness, the face becoming rounder (doctors call this "facial mooning"), and the development of acne. As the dose continues to be reduced, so do most of prednisone's symptoms.

◉ Immunosuppressives

These medications suppress the immune system and reduce inflammation. Side effects can include lowering of the body's overall ability to fight infection.

◉ Antibiotics

These medications reduce infections and inflammation.

Most people with IBD take either sulfasalazine or prednisone (corticosteroid). Both medicines help to reduce the inflammation in the body caused by IBD. At times, strong antibiotics are also used. Newer drugs like immunosuppressives are occasionally used. Doctors may also prescribe medications to help control diarrhea and abdominal pain, and recommend supplemental vitamins and minerals. Sometimes the side effects do not merit taking a particular drug and another one may be recommended, or your doctor might have to experiment with the dosage to find the correct medication and level for your body. With prednisone, you may be advised to cut out foods that are high in salt, like potato chips and pretzels.

I had to go on prednisone. I did not like the side effects. I retained water. I put on a lot of weight. It makes you have an increased appetite. I was really moody. Recently, I was sick again and the doctor recommended prednisone. I would not go on it again because of the side effects. I am sixteen, and appearance means a lot to me. I told my doctor I would rather have the pain.

Several drugs are helpful in controlling Crohn's disease, but at this point there continues to be no cure. The usual goals of therapy are to correct nutritional deficiencies, to control inflammation, and to relieve abdominal pain, diarrhea, and rectal bleeding. The drug sulfasalazine lessens the inflammation, especially in the colon. This drug can be used as long as needed, and it can be used along with other drugs. Side effects occur in a small percentage of cases. Patients who cannot tolerate this drug often do better on related drugs known as mesalamine or 5-ASA agents. More serious cases may require steroid drugs, antibiotics, or drugs that affect the body's immune system, such as azathioprine or 6-mercaptopurine (6-MP). No special diet has been proven effective for preventing or treating Crohn's disease. Some people cannot tolerate milk, alcohol, spices, or fiber.

People with ulcerative colitis may also be first treated with 5-ASA agents, which help to control inflammation. Again, sulfasalazine is the most commonly used of these drugs. People with severe cases of ulcerative colitis may be treated with corticosteroids (prednisone and hydrocortisone). These drugs can be given orally, intravenously, by enema, or in a suppository form depending on where the inflammation is. Because of the side effects of medications, your doctor should be monitoring your drugs closely.

Before we complete the discussion of medications, here are some important reminders. Always ask your doctor what a medication is and what it is for. Ask what the potential side effects are and which ones should be of major concern. List all the medications, vitamins, aspirin, and other drugs that you currently take and ask the doctor whether this new medication will interfere with any of the others. Ask if the medication can be taken with food and if there are foods or liquids to avoid. Ask your doctor when the medication will "kick in"— in other words, will it be effective immediately, or will it take effect days, weeks, or even months after taking it. Ask whether there are any alternatives that you can take if necessary. Ask how long you will need to be on the medication. See if there is any literature, pamphlets, or studies to help you truly understand the medication.

Finally, there are no silly questions, so be comfortable when talking to your doctor.

Surgery

Many people of all ages ask if they will need an operation when they are told they have IBD. Surgery might be recommended if the medications are not working or if you are having severe complications. If you are not growing properly, this may be another reason for your doctor to recommend surgery. Sometimes young people begin to catch up on their growth after the diseased part of their intestine has been removed. The need for surgery is discussed with your doctor, and all questions and concerns should always be addressed before you take this step. It is important for a teenager to be part of the conversation. It is still your body that will be affected, so you must be comfortable with the decisions that are affecting your life. Some operations are simple and can be completed in a doctor's office. An example of a simple operation is when pimples or cuts on the buttocks become filled with infected fluid. The fluid is drained and the opening is closed surgically.

Some operations require going to the hospital. Crohn's disease can make the bowel become thicker and thicker, until there is a possibility of obstruction. A surgeon can unblock the bowel, making it wider and therefore

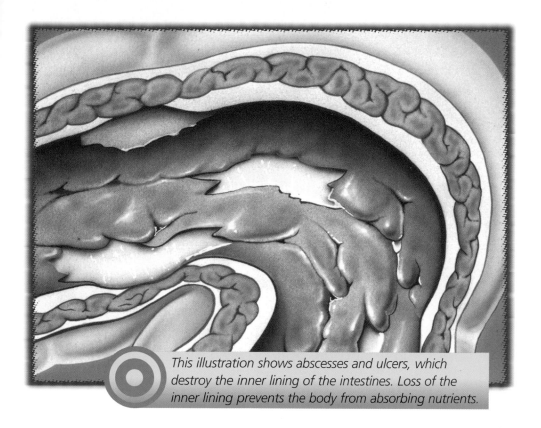

This illustration shows abscesses and ulcers, which destroy the inner lining of the intestines. Loss of the inner lining prevents the body from absorbing nutrients.

allowing the body to have a proper bowel movement. There are times when it becomes necessary to remove a section of the bowel. For example, if a person has Crohn's disease in which a section of the bowel has been infected, the surgeon removes the diseased section and sews together the remaining bowel. This is called a resection. Even though the person may feel better after having the resection, this is not a cure for Crohn's disease, since the disease often comes back in a different part of the intestine after the operation.

If surgery is necessary for ulcerative colitis, the surgeon removes the entire large intestine (a colectomy).

The operation changes the way a person uses the toilet. The bowel waste empties into an appliance (a disposable bag) worn on the lower front part of the body. This new opening is called an ileostomy. Again, hearing this for the first time is fairly traumatic. But talking to people who have disposable bags reveals that most of them adjust well and are able to lead completely normal lives. Newer operations have been developed in which a special "pouch" is created inside the body to collect waste. This, therefore, makes wearing an outside bag unnecessary. It is imperative that both the bag and the pouch be emptied several times during the day. Once the colon is removed in ulcerative colitis, the disease is cured.

I knew a man who had ulcerative colitis and had a bag put in when he was a teenager. He was upset, terribly embarrassed, and concerned for his future. Well, he is married now and has children of his own. It was not the end of the world for him!

Diagnosis

Unfortunately, IBD is usually diagnosed only after you have experienced such severe symptoms that the doctors need to investigate. To figure out for certain if you

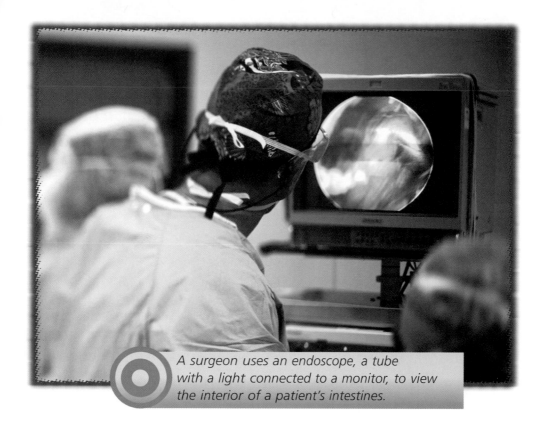

A surgeon uses an endoscope, a tube with a light connected to a monitor, to view the interior of a patient's intestines.

have IBD, you will probably have to go to a hospital or clinic to have medical tests done. Some of the tests you may have are X rays using barium and a sigmoidoscopy or colonoscopy. A barium X ray of the colon is a procedure that involves filling the colon with barium, a chalky white solution. The barium shows up white on X-ray film, allowing the doctor a clear view of the colon. The doctor may also do a colonoscopy, which is a test where the doctor inserts an endoscope—a long, flexible, lighted tube connected to a computer and TV monitor—into your anus and views the inside of your colon and rectum. Although these tests are not pleasant, they are a way for your doctor to determine which part of your intestine is inflamed and therefore how to treat it. It may be necessary to repeat these tests from time to time to see how you are responding to treatment or to see if the flare-up relocates. Once in a while, you will probably have to get blood samples taken. This may be done to see if a medication is working or to see if the body is getting all the proper nutrients it needs. This is especially important for children who have IBD, in order to make sure that they remain healthy and continue their growth process.

If you have experienced chronic abdominal pain, diarrhea, fever, weight loss, and symptoms of anemia, your doctor will examine you for Crohn's disease. The doctor will take a history and give you a thorough physical exam. The exam will include blood tests to find out if you are anemic as a result of the blood loss, or if there is an increased number of white blood cells, suggesting an inflammation in your body. Examination of a stool sample can tell the doctor if there is blood loss, or if an infection by a parasite or bacteria is causing the symptoms. The doctor may look inside your rectum and colon through a flexible tube (an endoscope) that is inserted through the anus. During the exam, the doctor might take a sample of tissue, called a biopsy, from the lining of the colon to look at under the microscope. You might receive X-ray examinations of the digestive tract to determine the nature and extent of the disease. These exams can include an upper gastrointestinal series, a small intestinal study, and a barium enema intestinal X ray. If you have Crohn's disease, you might need medical care for a long time. Your doctor will also want to test you regularly to check on your condition.

For ulcerative colitis, a series of tests may be required to diagnose the disease. Blood and stool samples are usually taken. Through a colonoscopy, the doctor will see if there is any bleeding, ulcers, or inflammation on the colon wall. The doctor might take a biopsy. A barium enema X ray of the colon might be required.

It is important that you have your symptoms investigated and not go a long time without getting medical assistance. Most, if not all, tests are done on an outpatient basis and you do not need to wait long for results. The sooner you are diagnosed, the sooner the healing can begin.

Chapter 3

Coping with the Stress

I don't cry about it. It is part of my life. I do not let it affect my life. Life hands you what it hands you, and I just take it. It is not a big deal in my life and I don't want it to be.

It is a chronic illness, but I do not think about it. I am positive, and right now it is under control. It has not held me back from travel and work.

You may have a lot of confusing and conflicting feelings about your disease. You might feel guilty or embarrassed, and sometimes you may feel very sad and even depressed when you are sick with IBD. You might be angry that you are feeling so much pain while others look like they are enjoying their lives with very few difficulties.

Talking to others who suffer from IBD can help a person cope with the disease. Seek out a support group.

It is normal to feel down about these painful and embarrassing symptoms that you are experiencing. It is OK to feel badly about having IBD. The drugs you are taking may affect your moods as well.

Sometimes you might feel that there is no one out there who truly understands how you feel both physically and emotionally. It may be time to find someone you can talk to in order to express your feelings. If you are comfortable with your parents, start there. Perhaps a close friend can be your support. If not, confiding these feelings to your doctor may be the impetus for you to get support from a psychologist or psychiatrist. There may be IBD support groups in your town or city. They might meet on occasion to talk among themselves. The IBD organizations usually include people who have the disease and can talk to you knowledgeably because they share your symptoms. Sometimes it is difficult to tell people you have IBD. Some people remain ignorant and can be insensitive, while others are very empathetic to your needs. You should be the one to decide how much you want to talk about your health and whom you want to talk to. If you are absent a lot from school, or if you have to go into the hospital, you or a parent should inform the school and explain the situation. Many people with IBD say that they just live with it. They do not let the disease define them. Sometimes they feel great, and there are times they feel bad. They also learn what to do and what not to do to make themselves feel better. They learn to manage their disease until it becomes part of their day-to-day life.

I always feel it could be so much worse. It is hell while you are experiencing the symptoms, but then you can forget. The more you complain and focus on it, the more you dwell on it. You have to live life the best you can.

Coping with IBD

Here are some strategies to help you cope with IBD in your daily life:

Though there is no cure, young people who suffer from IBD can lead normal and active lives.

◉ **Educate yourself.** The more you know about and understand your condition, the better you can manage and understand what your body is going through. It is more stressful to remain ignorant.

◉ **Eat well.** It is vital that you eat nutritious, well-balanced meals. It is important for your physical and mental growth.

◉ **Exercise.** You should be as active as you feel like being. There is no reason why you can't take part in most sports. An energizing activity relieves stress by

Even athletic activities, such as swimming, are possible for IBD sufferers.

releasing soothing endorphins throughout your body. If you are experiencing severe IBD symptoms, you may need to take a day or more off school and try to relax.

◉ Relax. There are many relaxation techniques. Some involve deep breathing, stretching, yoga, and meditation. Here is a meditative exercise you can try. Create a quiet place. Sit comfortably with both feet touching the ground. Close your eyes. Pause a moment. Begin to be aware of your breathing. Inhale. Exhale. Allow each inhalation to be slower and longer in duration. Pause before you exhale. Allow your body to sink deeper into the chair. As you relax, your body will feel heavier and very still. If your mind begins to wander, pay attention to your breathing. Continue this as long as you are able to. Some days it will be a half hour; other days it will be five minutes. As you end your meditation, you feel yourself almost awakening. Sit still for a moment. Take several deep breaths. At any point during the day, remember how good you felt during your meditation.

◉ Empower yourself. Be your own health advocate. Understand the benefits of monitoring your own medication. Be prepared with questions to ask your doctor when you have your checkup.

◉ Set your priorities. Ask yourself what is important. Learn to say no sometimes. Complete the tougher tasks when you have more energy. When you are low in energy, take the time to regroup. It is OK to ask for help.

◎ Join a support group. There are many support groups all over the world for Crohn's disease and ulcerative colitis. The Internet can also connect you to people who have IBD. These groups can support you and assure you that you are not alone with your disease.

◎ Talk to a professional. Sometimes you might need to make an appointment with a psychiatrist, psychologist, social worker, or guidance counselor. You might need someone to help you with your stress or someone to open up to in confidence.

Some General Guidelines

When in school, here are some things to think about:

◎ Always keep a change of clothes in your locker.

◎ A list of medications should be given to the principal's office.

◎ A list of emergency contact numbers should be given to the principal's office.

◎ Arrange with your teacher for a seat next to the door, in case you need to go to the rest room in a hurry.

- Know where the rest rooms are located at school and on field trips.

- If you need to be hospitalized, inform the school so that your teachers can be flexible about your homework, tests, and exams.

- Wear a medical alert bracelet.

- Eat properly.

- Remember to take your medications at the correct time each day.

Here are some nutritious and fun recipes to try when you are not feeling severe symptoms:

Berry Yogurt Shake

1 cup (250 ml) whole milk

1/3 cup (80 ml) frozen blueberries, raspberries, or strawberries

1/4 cup (180 ml) yogurt

(Note: You can use lactaid products)

Mix all ingredients together in a blender or food processor. It should be mixed until smooth.

Greek Salad

1 head romaine lettuce, shredded

1 red onion, chopped

2 medium tomatoes, cut up (or use cherry tomatoes)

1 cucumber

1/2 cup–1 cup (125 ml–250 ml) crumbled feta cheese

black or Greek olives to taste

Dressing: Mix oil, balsamic vinegar, salt, garlic, pepper, basil, and oregano

Add ingredients together in a wooden bowl.

Baked Triple Cheese Omelet

2 eggs, beaten

1 cup (250 ml) cottage cheese

1/2 cup (125 ml) grated cheddar cheese

Parmesan cheese, salt, pepper, dill, to taste

Preheat oven to 350 degrees. Grease an oven dish. In a bowl combine eggs and cottage cheese. Pour into oven dish. Sprinkle the top with the cheddar and Parmesan cheeses. Bake for ten minutes.

Future Research

Why has a cure for IBD not been discovered? Basic research into IBD involves meticulous work that progresses in very small sequential steps. In a laboratory, scientists have the ability to isolate a single variable, study it, study what changes occur in the intestine during inflammation, and how certain drugs reduce the inflammation. Here are what some people are studying in the latest research on IBD:

◉ **Immune Wars: Recent advances in immunological research, now being applied to IBD, suggest a growing connection between the skirmishes within the immune system and sufferers of Crohn's disease and ulcerative colitis. Experimental therapies that target the immune system are showing significant promise.**

◉ **Virtual Reality: Researchers are exploring new ways to apply a form of computer technology, known as virtual reality, to medical diagnosis. Virtual colonoscopy would allow doctors to view a three-dimensional simulation of a person's organs. This may eventually aid in tracking the progress of IBD.**

◉ **Nicotine: In some people, nicotine seems to have a preventative effect against the development of ulcerative colitis but a detrimental effect in Crohn's disease.**

◎ **New Drugs: On average, it takes twelve years and costs $359 million to put a new drug on the market. Pharmaceutical companies, scientists, members of the medical profession, and government agencies are constantly doing research on new medications.**

◎ **Appendix: Recent studies are suggesting a link between the appendix and ulcerative colitis. Could it be that by removing the appendix people will be protected from developing ulcerative colitis? The research continues.**

It is important for you to understand that research is constantly going on to discover the causes of and a cure for IBD. It is also imperative that you do not believe everything you read and hear, especially on the Internet. There are many Web sites claiming cures. Every disease, including IBD, has had its fad "cures" and therapies. Check with your family doctor before jeopardizing your health. Many cures and therapies may be just money-makers, and the buyer needs to be aware of the pitfalls.

There is no doubt that Crohn's disease and ulcerative colitis are not easy diseases to live with. There is no warning when these diseases will flare up, and you may feel incapacitated when they do. With modern medicines,

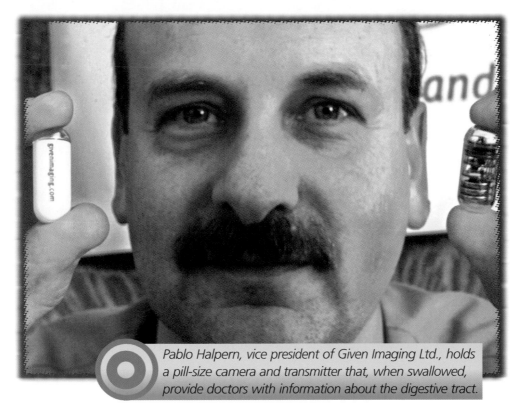

Pablo Halpern, vice president of Given Imaging Ltd., holds a pill-size camera and transmitter that, when swallowed, provide doctors with information about the digestive tract.

most symptoms can be treated. The disease will not go away, but you can learn to live with it. Each day brings us closer to discovering the cause of IBD. Once the cause is known, maybe the cure will shortly follow.

I still play all sports, have an active life, and do my own thing. A lot of research is going on. Maybe there will be a cure in my lifetime.

Glossary

abscess A pocket or collection of pus. In IBD, abscesses typically form in the abdominal cavity or rectal area.

anemia Iron deficiency and decreased amounts of hemoglobin in red blood cells.

anus The opening of the anal canal, at the end of the rectum.

barium enema An X-ray examination of the colon and sometimes the end of the ileum, using a suspension of barium sulfate that appears white on exposed X-ray film.

biopsy A tissue sample removed for examination under a microscope. An entire section can be removed or only a little bit.

chronic Recurring or occurring over a long period of time.

colectomy Surgical removal of the colon.

colitis Inflammation of the colon, or large intestine.

colon The large intestine.

colonoscopy An examination of the colon with a flexible instrument inserted into the rectum.

diarrhea Bowel movements that are softer, looser, or more frequent than normal.

duodenum The first part of the small intestine, starting at the lower end of the stomach and extending to the jejunum.

endoscope An instrument used to examine the inside of the body.

endoscopy A direct examination of the interior of the digestive tract using a fiber-optic endoscope.

false urge A strong but mistaken feeling that a bowel movement is going to occur. It is a symptom of rectal inflammation.

feces Waste matter excreted from the bowel consisting of unabsorbed foods, water, bacteria, and intestinal secretions.

fissure A crack or crevice in the skin surrounding the anus.

fistulas An abnormal opening between two loops of intestine, or the intestine and another structure such as the bladder.

gastroenterologist A medical specialist in the diagnosis and treatment of diseases of the stomach, intestines, and associated organs.

ileostomy A surgically created opening of the ileum to the abdominal wall, allowing the diversion of fecal waste.

irritable bowel syndrome (IBS) A disorder of the gastrointestinal tract usually involving an abnormal bowel habit and abdominal discomfort. IBS can mimic some features of Crohn's disease but does not usually cause weight loss.

jejunum The upper portion of the small intestine, connecting the duodenum to the ileum.

lactose A naturally occurring sugar found in dairy products.

lactose intolerance A condition caused by a decrease or absence of the enzyme lactase, which aids in the digestion of milk sugar (lactose).

obstruction A blockage. An obstruction of the small or large intestine prevents the normal passage of intestinal contents.

perforation The formation of a hole. Perforation of the bowel wall allows the intestinal contents to enter the peritoneal cavity.

remission A reduction of symptoms and a return to good health.

resection The surgical removal of a diseased portion of an organ or structure.

sigmoidoscopy An examination of the rectum and sigmoid colon with an endoscope.

stool The fecal discharge from the bowel.

tube feeding The delivery of nutrients to the gastrointestinal tract through a tube.

ulcerative colitis Another type of inflammatory bowel disease that affects only the colon.

For More Information

Crohn's & Colitis Foundation of America (CCFA)
National Headquarters
386 Park Avenue South, 17th Floor
New York, NY 10016-8894
(800) 932-2423
Web site: http://www.ccfa.org

Crohn's and Colitis Foundation of Canada
60 St. Clair Avenue East, Suite 600
Toronto, ON M4T 1N5
Canada
(416) 920-5035
(800) 387-1479
Web site: http://www.ccfc.ca

Web Sites

Due to the changing nature of Internet links, the Rosen Publishing Group, Inc., has developed an online list of Web sites related to the subject of this book. The site is updated regularly. Please use this link to access the list:

http://www.rosenlinks.com/ntk/crdc

For Further Reading

Gomez, Joan. *Positive Options for Crohn's Disease*.
    Almeda, CA: Hunter House Inn, 2000.

Greenwood, Jan K. *The IBD Nutrition Book*. New
    York: John Wiley & Sons, 1992.

Saibul, Fred. *Crohn's Disease & Ulcerative Colitis*.
    Toronto: Key Porter Books Ltd., 1996.

Stein, Stanley, and Richard Rood. *Inflammatory Bowel
    Disease*. Philadelphia: Lippincott-Raven
    Publishers, 1999.

Trachter, Amy B. *Coping with Crohn's Disease*.
    Oakland, CA: New Harbinger, 2001.

Bibliography

Harper, Virginia M. *Controlling Crohn's Disease: The Natural Way*. New York: Kensington Publishers, 2002.

Kyle, James. *Crohn's Disease*. London: Heinemann Medical, 1972.

Lichtenstein, Gary R., ed. *The Clinician's Guide to Inflammatory Bowel Disease*. Thorofare, NJ: Slack, 2003.

Pilkington, Robert R. *The Complete Crohnie Handbook: A Comprehensive Guide for the Crohn's Disease Patient*. Scottsdale, AZ: Wolftracks Publishers, 2002.

Zonderman, Jon, and Ronald Vender. *Understanding Crohn's Disease and Ulcerative Colitis*. Oxford, MS: University Press of Mississippi, 2000.

Index

A

abdominal pain, 13, 15, 16, 17, 33, 34, 40
anemia, 16, 17, 40
antibiotics, 33, 34
anus, 10, 12, 13, 14, 16, 17, 18, 23, 39, 40
appendix, 14

B

biopsy, 40, 41
bleeding, 7, 15, 16, 21, 34
bowel movement, 12, 16, 37
bowels, 10–12, 14, 17, 23, 28, 36–38

C

colectomy, 37–38
colon, 10, 12, 14–15, 17, 23, 34, 38, 39, 40
    cancer of, 25
colonoscopy, 39, 41, 51
corticosteroids, 33, 35

Crohn, Burrill, 13
Crohn's colitis, 7, 14
Crohn's disease
    about, 13–14
    causes of, 19–20
    and children, 20, 22–23
    complications of, 22–23, 25
    diagnosis of, 40–41
    history of, 12–13
    and medication, 34
    and remission, 14
    and surgery, 36–37
    symptoms of, 7, 13–14, 16, 17

D

digestive system, how it works, 9–12
distal colitis, 7, 15
duodenum, 10, 14

E

esophagus, 10, 14

F

false urge, 16–17
fever, 7, 14, 16, 40
5-aminosalicylate (5-ASA), 32,
    34, 35
food/diet
    to avoid diarrhea, 30
    to avoid gas, 29
    sensitivity/allergy to,
        18, 21, 25
    to treat IBD, 28–30

G

gastroenterologist, 27
gastrointestinal (GI) tract,
    9, 13
glucocorticosteroids, 32–33

H

hydrocortisone, 35

I

ileitis, 7, 14
ileocolitis, 14
ileostomy, 38
ileum, 10, 13, 14, 23
immune system, 19, 20–21,
    33, 51
immunosuppressives, 33
inflammatory bowel
        disease (IBD)
    causes of, 18–21
    complications of, 21–26
    coping with, 42–50
    degrees of, 18
    diagnosis of, 38–41
    and medication, 21, 23, 25,
        26, 27, 31–36, 43, 52–53
    other names for, 7

research into, 50–52
seeking help for, 26
and teens/children, 12,
    20, 22, 23, 40
treating, 27–41
where it's prevalent, 9

J

jejunum, 10
joint pain, 14, 15, 16, 25

L

large intestine (large bowel),
    10–12, 14, 37

M

medication, 21, 23, 25, 26, 27,
    31–36, 43, 52–53
mouth, 10, 13, 14, 17

P

pancolitis, 7, 15
prednisone, 28, 32–33, 35

R

recipes, 49–50
rectum, 10, 12, 14–15, 16, 17,
    39, 40
resection of bowel, 37

S

small intestine (small bowel),
    10, 12, 13, 14
stomach, 10, 14, 28–29
stress, 18, 20, 21
sulfasalazine, 31–32, 33, 34
support, getting, 43–44, 48
surgery, 17, 21, 23, 27,
    36–38

T

toxic megacolon, 23

U

ulcerative colitis
    about, 14–15
    causes of, 20–21
    complications of, 23–25

diagnosis of, 41
    and medication, 35
    and surgery, 37–38
    symptoms of, 7, 16–17
ulcerative proctitus, 15

W

weight loss, 14, 16, 17, 22, 40

About the Authors

Sandra Giddens, Ed.D., and Owen Giddens, Ph.D., reside in Toronto with their two children, Justine and Kyle. Sandra is a special education consultant and Owen is director of Rehabilitation Counseling Services in Toronto. They would especially like to thank Sarah, Faye, and the Crohn's and Colitis Foundation of Canada for their excellent input into this book.

Photo Credits

Cover, p. 22 © Superstock; p. 2 © John Henley/Corbis; pp. 8, 11, 24, 37 © Custom Medical; p. 39 © Robert Llewellyn/Corbis; pp. 43, 45, 46 © Index Stock; p. 53 © Reuters New Media/Corbis.

Design

Thomas Forget

Layout

Hillary Arnold